Tucked Away in a Discolored Scrapbook: Creative Nonfiction with Poetry

S.V. Farnsworth

Published by Stone Wolfe Press, 2022.

While every precaution has been taken in the preparation of this book, the publisher assumes no responsibility for errors or omissions, or for damages resulting from the use of the information contained herein.

TUCKED AWAY IN A DISCOLORED SCRAPBOOK: CREATIVE NONFICTION WITH POETRY

First edition. April 23, 2022.

ISBN: 978-1733859950

Written by S.V. Farnsworth.

Also by S.V. Farnsworth

Fusion in a Fission World
Hard Start: Mars Intrigue
Tidal Pulse: Mars Revolution

Modutan Empire
Woman of the Stone
Monarch in the Flames

Standalone
A Rare Connection: Inspirational Romantic Suspense
Tucked Away in a Discolored Scrapbook: Creative Nonfiction
with Poetry

Watch for more at https://svfarnsworthauthor.com.

Table of Contents

To the remarkable women of my family and the wonderful men who love them.

Pickers

I cannot explain time, but I had more of it when I was younger. Tucked away in a discolored scrapbook is a Polaroid picture of me as a small girl sitting on a petrified stump the diameter of a VW Bug. The picture is taken from the side, so the redwood forest is out of frame behind me and the ocean waves beneath the gray clouds of dawn are in view.

The wind blows through my sun-bleached hair, wet with sea spray. Surrounded by all this raw nature, I have such a solemn expression on my face. What was going through my toddler mind? I think I was simply soaking up the wild beauty and reveling in a profound state of being. The feeling remains, forever at the core of me. It's who I am.

Such moments once composed the whole of my life. There are dozens of faded photos in my mother's picture albums. A little girl by a stream with a stick. My smiling face is at the forefront among the presidents of Mount Rushmore. I've visited places other people rarely do. How then did I end up like them, chained to one place?

For years, I blamed the birth of my baby brother for my family's change of pace. We had been free spirits but settled in a house with a yard and a dog. Two young children were too many for my parents to live a transient lifestyle, not when my grandparents offered stability. However, I cannot help but feel the loss of freedom even now. Where I was once at full liberty of both mind and body, I am now partially blocked. Being reasonable can exact a heavy price.

Orphans who stare at nothing but white walls from birth can't see color later in life. What did I see as a child? What did I miss? Back then, I could easily incorporate new aspects of life into myself. But if I didn't do so then, as a child, then it is likely I don't even know what is absent today. It's difficult to fundamentally alter one's self as an adult, but not impossible.

I can break free of prime-time TV and instead watch the stars come out in the night sky. It's possible to learn to tolerate the insects, the humidity, and the temperature swings, accepting them until I feel grounded. I can connect with the heaven that enlightens me. I can adjust when I see value in it.

I've made changes. Not all of them are good. I live in a house now, instead of a camper shell on an old pickup truck. Back when the Polaroid picture of me on the petrified stump was taken, my mother picked fruits and vegetables while my father worked odd carpentry jobs. We traveled from Mexico to Canada along the Pacific coastline. But creature comforts have a way of wriggling into our lives. I guess that's fine as I age and time passes me by.

I have eaten the inedible produce from the grocery store, wincing each time I check out. I pay a price for what my parents gave up to live within four walls. Their marriage collapsed inside those walls. Yet, I still know strawberries are puffed juice warmed by the sun, and blueberries taste like a grin. Don't pucker your face. You'd likely feel the same way I do if you have ever had sun-ripened food picked with your own hands.

Start the seeds. Plant a garden. Wait ten years for an orchard to grow. Pull a gazillion weeds. Eat a pathway through a happy life like an inchworm wearing a straw hat.

Time-consuming? Impossible in a busy world? Perhaps, but when I was younger, I had more time. Every moment was a golden gift filled with wonder. Now my porch chair encourages me to slumber. And as I drift away, I consider the accomplishments of my life. Most of them don't sway in the moonlight like pecan trees, zucchini jungles, and fireflies, but nature's symphony of infinite tomorrows might just stir me to arise and dance.

Astern

A little girl with her mother's eyes.
Look out the back window of your rolling home.
Volkswagen bug of stalled aspiration.
See the world.
Lives lived in passing.
No roots, but one.
Grandma's hands, pulling in, pulling back.
Old strength to young growth.
Stretch and thrive before you drive.
Away.

Milk Jug

S omewhere in the daydream that encompasses the age of four, I was playing in the yard on a sunny day. It was not too hot and not too cold. Thirsty, I ran inside for a glass of milk.

Mom said we didn't have any, and I asked if we could buy some. She said we didn't have enough gas in the car. I knew what that meant. However, being a resourceful child, I thought I could fix the problem.

Formulating a plan, I asked for the empty milk jug and trotted outside. With careful measurements, I mixed water and dirt until it looked like gas. I unscrewed the gas cap and poured my solution into the tank, then turned the cap and closed the flap. Unfortunately, the drizzle of sand on the side of the car made me think something wasn't right.

Looking at the jug in my hand, I remembered earlier today when I'd added water to the last of the milk to make more. Mom had been mad. She'd explained that I hadn't made more milk, but ruined what we had left. Peering into the jug at the dregs of dirt in the bottom, I became quite certain I was in trouble.

I didn't want to be around to see how angry Mom became over this. So, I hid the jug in a bush and walked casually inside. I asked for a paper sack and headed to my room to pack clothes.

My baby brother followed me. Since I didn't want him to be scolded for my mistake, I took him by the hand. We marched through the kitchen to the great outdoors.

We didn't stop in the yard or the dirt driveway but turned left onto a grassy roadside. Surrounded by pastures, we headed along the road toward the only other house in sight. Soon Mom called for us, but we didn't answer.

Before long, the nose of our rust-colored bug pulled up to the end of the drive. I quickly urged my brother to hide in the tall grass. We watched Mom zoom past, and as soon as she disappeared, we continued onward.

At last, we reached a house down the road. When we knocked on the door, a kindly woman answered and let us in. We sat on her couch with our hastily packed clothes.

The woman gave us milk and cookies while she called our mother. When Mom came, I just knew I'd be spanked, but instead, she hugged and hugged us. She thanked the woman, and we three walked home. The car's engine had blown.

Grandma Lilly's Backyard

A gentle breeze carried the apricot blossoms' perfume to my senses as I stepped out the back door of Grandma and Grandpa Lilly's house. My little brother and I loved to play in Grandma's backyard. He played trucks on the walkway, and I lay in the grass watching the swiftly moving stratus-level clouds. I liked the way they shielded the black lava hills from the scorching heat of the sun.

Even in the spring, the weather was hot in the small Southern Utah town. The thick, cool grass was a deep, hardy green. The fresh-cut smell intoxicated my energetic young body and mind to heights of imagination I'd never had time to explore before.

The rustling of leaves in an enormous walnut tree distracted me. A shift in the air currents swayed the branches of a silver maple next to it. They offered the luxury of shade on the north side of the yard, and I moved into it for relief.

A cement walkway bisected the grass, heading east toward the barn. It was a half-barn, containing a push lawnmower, a rotor-tiller, sawhorses, and most of Grandpa's useful equipment and tools. Just for me, it also housed a nanny goat with two kids. I needed the milk.

The south side of the yard had two trees as well, a young pear and a prime apricot. That old tree bore thousands of apricots each year. I helped grandma gather them into buckets, wash them in the kitchen, and can them in fruit jars. There is nothing in the world like the taste of sun-ripened apricots with the juice running down my arms.

A volcanic rock wall raised the level of a section of the yard along the south fence by about three feet. In the center lay a huge, gray boulder capped with a crown of blooming cacti. The long white needles and fuzzy prickles warned me not to climb, but I seldom listened.

Grandma washed my cactus-pricked hands so gently. Then she ruthlessly sprayed my wounds with Bactine. The sting of the antiseptic made me wince but didn't stop me from climbing that huge rock again.

Grandpa built everything, including the house, but not the cactus-covered boulder. His loving hands had constructed the yard around that Godly creation. Even for a man of his patient might, some things, like Grandma, remained immovable.

My grandma, my grandpa, my mother, and my little brother existed in the radiant sunlight and starry moonlight of that backyard. I came to understand unconditional love there. Wrapped in an unending string of why questions, I learned many things.

My family shaped my world in that backyard. It symbolizes heaven to me. It is the place where everything makes sense and every question has an answer.

Earliest Memory

My first memory is as vivid as a brilliant blue sky over orange dunes relieved with desert sage. It is as inviting as the rays of the sun and as innocuous as a bright green highway sign, and yet the dialogue makes all the difference. "I killed a woman and buried her out there." The dialogue is what caused my memory to awaken for the first time and my father's lack of a response to what the other man said is what made me who I am.

What is my earliest memory? It isn't happy. I'm sure I had plenty of those, but they don't leave a mark.

The first thing I remember had to be when I was at the age of two because my mom was pretty big with my baby brother. My parents and I were in a truck with a big bench seat. Dad wasn't driving, another man was. Dad sat beside him with me to his right and Mom asleep against the passenger side door.

I remember looking up when the man told my dad to look out the driver's side window. The man had it rolled down. He stretched his long arm, pointing at some red dunes with short red sandstone bluffs behind them.

"I killed a woman and buried her out there," the man said.

I climbed up on my dad's knee to see. I looked at my dad, but he didn't say anything. I glanced ahead on the two-lane highway, spotting a mile marker and a big green sign, but I couldn't read them.

I wanted the woman found and the man put in jail. He was bigger than my dad, taller in the seat and broader in the shoulders. He was white, with dark brown hair and a smile on his face. He had nice teeth.

Finally, I turned to my mom. I tried to wake her, but she was too exhausted. She wasn't any help.

I don't remember anything else. Except that this event, as I remember it, changed my life. My dad didn't laugh, or smile, but he didn't stand up for that woman.

It had been easy for that other man to kill her, brag about it, and get away with it. I understood completely that I wasn't worth anything because I was a girl. I carried this with me my whole life and it changed me.

After I married, I told my husband about what I remembered. He said, "I wouldn't have said anything either, not with my wife and babies in the truck with a murderer." The insight surprised me.

I've thought a lot about it. I'd like to think that my dad called the police. That the woman's body was found, and the man was imprisoned for life.

I know that most decent people would have made sure that happened if they could, but my dad wasn't a decent man. I'm pretty sure that he drank, drugged, and cheated that memory away. And I'm afraid to ask him now that he's sometimes sober. I don't know him well enough to speak so frankly.

I like to think of myself as being brave. I like to think that I would do the right thing. I haven't done it yet.

Time

The fleeting moment of time
When the wind blows
And the sun shines.
The trees will sway,
And the grass will grow,
And time will simply flow.

Grandpa Lilly

Rex Alton Lilly had a habit of saving his chewing gum behind his earlobe when eating lunch or speaking on the telephone. I could always see it because he buzzed short what little hair he had with electric clippers. As a kid, I loved the feel of his soft, spiky hair.

He would always say, "Don't mess it up!" and laugh as I tried.

He had dimples just like me. I ought to mention he was my grandmother's second husband. He was not related to me by blood, just in every other way.

I remember a picture of Grandpa as a young man. He had sleek dark hair, trim, with a pert part near the middle. I thought he was so handsome. I guess he laughed about me messing up his hair because, in his younger years, he took great pains to look sharp. He probably even carried a comb in his back pocket.

Grandpa was a ballplayer, a basketball coach to be exact. He taught me how to hold a basketball and shoot. He taught me to dribble and pass. I loved basketball because he did.

Even though I was the only girl on my fourth-grade team in Sacramento, California, my team won a trophy taller than I was. I wish I had a picture. I only warmed the bench that one year.

When Grandpa wasn't in a suit and tie headed out on church-related activities, he wore bib overalls and worked in the yard or at the farm. I loved the farm. He had a pecan and pistachio farm when I was growing up.

We'd take his pickup truck to the farm unless Grandma was coming, then we'd drive the car. It was southeast of Mesquite, Nevada. We'd drive forty miles an hour on washboard dirt roads, ten miles straight ahead and thirty miles up and down.

The glovebox always held chewing gum, Big Red or Juicy Fruit, and a box of toothpicks. Grandpa and Grandma kept all their teeth to the end. I think it must have been because of this.

Grandpa often had a toothpick in his mouth. In fact, his mouth was one of his most animated qualities. If ever I pouted about something, he would say, "Don't trip on that lip."

Truth be told, he often pursed out his lips as he eyeballed a measurement. Per Grandma's request, he would build another outbuilding at the farm or move the furniture around the house, always with his lips protruding. Thus, his lips were not just for smiling, but for thinking. I loved that. It was the one thing the funeral home got wrong for his viewing.

He always wore a straw hat "to create some shade" and carried a shovel as if it were an extension of his arm. He cut the roots out from under tumbleweeds, maintained tree rings, and occasionally cut the head off of rattlesnakes. I mostly played with rocks and marveled at the fold-up toilet seat that could be set up anywhere.

It affronted my modesty to go potty in the open. However, I secretly enjoyed the cool breeze on my bum after a hot day as I watched the setting sun. By the time I gathered the courage to go, it was usually time to head home.

My grandpa built his own houses to save money. He built cabinets during the summer to earn a little extra income. Working as a teacher only paid the bills nine months out of the year. So, when my mom was young, he built their house in Toquerville, Utah.

For many years, he used rock from the side of a nearby mountain for various things. I remember going with him once to the edge of a high cliff. He backed the truck up to the edge and used a prybar to flake off huge slabs of red sandstone.

I have no idea how he lifted that rock into the bed of his truck. But with trip after trip, he used the stone to finish the outside of the house. Then, he built a long retaining wall the entire length of the long driveway.

I helped him by eating purple mulberries while he mixed up mortar in his wheelbarrow with a flathead shovel. I lent him moral support by floating split okra boats in the irrigation ditch while he put the wall together one evening after another as we rotated water to the garden rows and flooded the orchard. We'd work until the mortar was used up, listening to frogs calling their evening songs as the stars came out in the darkening sky and the desert night cooled the radiant earth.

My mom, brother, and I lived with Grandma and Grandpa in that house in Toquerville for a short time. I was six. It was just after my parents separated.

I'd catch the bus at the same place my mother had while she was growing up. The stop lay at a little park with a tall metal slide and two swings. From the end of my grandparents' driveway, it was a couple of houses away.

My favorite mornings, however, were on the weekends. My little brother, Heath, and I would sneak downstairs from the pink room that had been my mother and aunt's bedroom as children. We'd run through the living room and dining area, past the bathroom, and into Grandma and Grandpa's room. We'd jump on the bed with them still asleep in it.

Grandpa would laugh and say, "Mercy, mercy!"

While Grandma went to make oatmeal or steamed rice with vanilla and sugar for breakfast, Grandpa would gather us up. With one of us on each side, he'd read the Scriptures. His voice was my favorite sound other than music.

He sang at church, we all did. The joy of it still thrills me today. He sang in earnest with deep power in his chest and so I learned to do that too, only soprano.

I sing all the time, this pop hit or that gospel hymn. Often, I just make up songs. I never could remember the words well anyway.

Grandpa's hands were rough from all that work. He had cut the tip off of two fingers on the planer, straightening out rough-cut wood to build that first house. Splinters of bone worked their way out for years.

I missed seeing the blood by being too young. However, I caught the cautionary tale. I have built furniture and machined a few tools. I love working with machinery and still have all my fingers.

I enjoyed seeing the world from half-size. Another early memory was at six or seven when Grandpa built their next home. They moved to St. George, Utah.

My brother and I played in the unfinished basement while Grandpa worked. Well, one day, he finished and took a shower in the downstairs bathroom. Dust wasn't allowed upstairs. Anyway, I wandered in unsuspecting.

"Where are you, Grandpa?" I twisted the knob and looked into the usually dark bathroom.

"I'm in the waste-paper basket," he said.

I walked past the shower curtain and sink to look into the little blue trashcan beside the stool.

"No, you're not, Grandpa," I said, but by then he had grabbed a towel.

Every minute with Grandpa was fun because of his quick wit and sense of humor. He made friends and influenced people wherever he went. He was always willing to lend a hand and eager to spend time with his children, grandchildren, and great-grandchildren.

He lived to be eighty-five. He beat prostate cancer and skin cancer, but in the end leukemia from the radiation treatments took his life. I think he survived so long because of all the watermelon he ate.

He grew as many watermelons as the varmints didn't take. He could thump a melon with his finger and tell if it was ripe or not. He never picked a bad one. There's nothing in the world like a ring of cold watermelon after a home-cooked meal.

I swallowed a melon seed once by accident, and Grandpa teased me that it would grow. I had such high hopes, but I eventually discovered that I have a black thumb. I try to plant or grow things and seldom have success. I often think of Grandpa and wish I could ask his advice.

Most years my family garden fails. The only reason I have flowering shrubs and pretty flower beds is that they were established when we bought our Missouri house. Fortunately, it rains enough to keep them alive.

From time to time my mother transplants something from her yard that I can't kill. She put in a whole row of Irises along my back fence. I enjoy their lavender elegance in the spring.

Grandpa sold the pecan farm and bought 20 acres of land in the opposite direction for dirt cheap. It was twenty acres of sand to be exact and located ten miles south of Apple Valley, Utah. The land was so far out in the middle of nowhere that it was off the electrical grid.

Every trip he made, he stopped at the horse track in Hurricane, Utah, to load his truck with free manure. I know, because I went with him as often as I could. Even then, he did it all a shovel full at a time.

He and Grandma bought a two-bedroom trailer for the farm so they could entertain the family in comfort. I thought that was odd since it took over an hour and required a truck or an SUV to drive the rocky road. Needless to say, they didn't have a lot of company at that farm.

Grandpa built a few sheds, put in a rotating solar array with battery storage, installed a water tank with a half horsepower pump, fenced in a garden, and set up rows for thornless blackberries. He did this all on handshake deals with local grocery store owners who said they would pay him a fair price and sell his produce. He had a lot of faith in people.

I traveled with him in my mid-twenties on the long trip to Texas to pick up the young vines. We talked and laughed there and back again as he taught me to drive his little, stick-shift pickup truck. He had so many stories to tell and such high hopes for those berries. Regardless of the best-laid plans, however, the farm only produced a profit when he sold it during the housing bubble.

He wore his life out with work. How he had the patience to always have children at his knee or elbow while he did it, I have no idea. I'm just grateful I was beside him as often as I was. I meet a person from time to time that reminds me of him, and that makes me miss him more than ever. Sometimes when I laugh, I sound like him. It's the best sound in the world.

Battle of the Grandmas

When I was eight years old, my mother remarried, making me accountable to my third set of grandparents. Amidst the laughter turned on me by my new extended family, I acquired the title of the redheaded step-child. I had never had adults laugh at my expense before. The humor held skepticism and suspicion, casting me in an unfavorable light. The poison of their words wormed into my shy heart and impressionable mind, swirling a new bitterness into my childhood.

My mother's family may be a bit mental, but we have one amazing quality going for us; we love. We give our love without holding back. On an equal note, we receive each other's love with joy.

Generosity is not our flaw. It's our strength. Do you need it? It's yours. No sacrifice is too much and no distance is too far to travel. No excuse ever stood in the way of Grandma and Grandpa Lilly.

My new grandparents were generous too, though they often attached conditions and harbored resentments. My stay-at-home mom and kind, hardworking step-dad sometimes needed help to make ends meet and put food on the table. As a child, I didn't understand their struggles.

I felt like my brother and I were "cash cows" used by my parents to milk money out of our grandparents. It was the worst kind of feeling. I didn't want to take advantage of anyone's kindness, but I needed the essentials of life.

My guilt increased when my mom never skipped a smoke. I felt obscured by her exhales as if my wants were blotted out by her addiction. Who was I compared to a cigarette?

Despite all the toxins my mother imbibed, she still loves with greater purity than anyone I know. My hurts don't compare to hers, nor my compassion for the defenseless. She speaks to animals, reads their minds, and knows their hearts. Nature's menagerie is far less beastly than people who have good intentions yet little love in their hearts. I learned that lesson the hard way.

Of all the wormy things I did to gain the respect of my Step-Grandma Clark, taking her side against my mom was the worst. It started little. A crystal candy dish in the parlor tempted me to partake of the forbidden treats my mother knew would send me into a rush of uninhibited frenzy and end in embarrassment. Cackles of laughter inevitably ensued, then the words, then our tears.

"Don't let the door hit you on the way out."

Never good enough.

Except that wasn't the conclusion of my story. Love knows no end, and my Grandma Lilly always made it better and worse and better again. Even now I can't help smiling as the memories flood back.

Grandma Lilly was my partner in crime, well, not in crime but we did have lots of fun. She always had a little money to splurge on an ice-cream cone or an occasional movie. Her fridge was filled with healthy things and her counter with fruits and vegetables grown at the farm with her own hands.

Grandma Clark's kitchen was a hub of industry and the center of the action. Rich stuff. I slunk through the crowd, avoiding attention, with my hand in the cookie jar at family dinners. We were made welcome in the most unwelcoming ways and always as an afterthought.

"Hot bread. Cold shoulder."

The word obligation is so ugly.

We moved almost as far as the Pacific Ocean would permit. Sacramento, California seemed like a land of opportunity to my naïve parents. Sure, my step-dad made good money, but it only bought marijuana, not piano lessons.

During my junior high school years, I called them out. They were the first to admit they were doing wrong, though it didn't change their behavior. Their guilt did afford me an "Anne of Green Gables" marathon on PBS from time to time, but only if the Indy 500 or the Preakness wasn't on the television.

I knew my place, though I didn't learn my value until I saw it in my Grandma Lilly's eyes every time she looked at me. I heard it in her voice when we talked on the phone. I felt it in the excited grasp of her hand taking mine on a walk around the block, breathing the night air as it descended with the fading of the sun. Grandma knew the power of good health. I wish I had remembered that my whole life.

There have been occasions when paralysis has overcome me, especially when I was a child. On the spot at Grandma Clark's was always one of those times. I never knew why I felt so insecure and nervous, but my anxiety definitely dropped my IQ to the level of her expectations.

I desperately wanted to please her, but that didn't happen until I married up. Oh, and I graduated from college. Suddenly, my husband and I were invited to the family reunion.

Grandma Clark's acceptance felt strange. I never managed to trust that it would last. To her credit, it did.

With Grandma Lilly, I never doubted my value for a single moment. I elevated my place in life because of her love. She inspired me in so many ways with the encouragement she gave me from my birth until her death.

I didn't ask for help often, but her safety net hugged me close many times as an adult. Her confidence in me made all the difference in my success. I occasionally wonder how people survive when strings are attached to everything they're ever given.

Transactions are never starker than when someone dies. Hordes of wealth unevenly dispensed to children is mercenary. It's as if the deceased has made their final bet.

Some of Grandma Clark's possessions fell to me. No one else wanted them, and it was easier to load my car with old clothes than to take them to the thrift store. Grandma Lilly had nothing left to give when she passed away. She had already given it all.

Red Cliffs Gray

Mist on red, ragged cliffs,
Flow, swirl, glide,
Collide with my vision,
Impact my sensibilities.
Gray backlit heavens,
Turn, lift, exhale,
Breathe liquid breath,
On my mourning mind.

Alcohol-Soaked DNA

Alcohol-soaked DNA, inherited, yet not acquired. It speaks to my mind with an enticingly, slurred speech. My ears understand it even without sound.

Alcohol is the undercurrent of American culture. It's often the underpinning of our society. Yet, I have never had a drink.

Do I think myself too good for the company? No. On the contrary, I feel the figurative sloshing in my belly.

I know that if I take one sip, make one slip, then I could lose everything. I'm one foot out of the gutter of addiction from whence my genes sprang. Wash as I may, the muddy choices of those who came before cling to me.

The mud reaches to my ears. Filth acquired by inheritance is the most unfair. Yet, it is a heritage I must escape.

I am the first. The first person in my family to remain sober. I never did any of it.

Admittedly, as a child, I inhaled the smoke-filled living room air. It floated so thick that I could hardly see the television. The silly smoke of green weed, worse than cigarettes for fouling up one's brain with tangent thoughts, made it very hard to ever reach a conclusion.

When did it end? When did the secrets end? Not until judgment ended. Not until I realized that most everyone other than me had done it, and most people couldn't care less what my parents smoked or drank.

So, I told. I betrayed some, not all, of what they said I should never repeat. The threat still looms, and I occasionally chew my nails in bed at night as I try to fall asleep, but now it's not for me.

I am safe. I thought I was safe, in my early twenties. I thought I had escaped the consequences of their sins by avoiding them myself, but I was wrong.

I did everything right and I am happy, but I suffer. I pay wages to the jilted master, addiction. The toll is my health.

Baleful, unrelenting pain and a Pandora's box of miseries never before seen in family history have landed on me. It's payback for daring to break the unbreakable chains of desolation. Regardless, I am free.

I graduated from a rural Missouri high school, the first on my father's side to earn a diploma. I served a full-time mission for eighteen months in South Korea, the first woman in my family to do so. I graduated from Southern Utah University, without, as Grandpa Clark said, a pot to pee in.

He was proud of me. He understood what that saying meant. In days long gone, tanners tanned leather with urine. If you were fortunate enough to have a pot, then at least you could sell what came naturally. If you didn't own a pot, then you were out of luck.

I may have been born out of luck, but determination seems to generate good fortune. I have never been satisfied with what's been handed to me. Rather, I've made choices and paid all of the necessary dues to follow my optimistic future.

Not many people believed in me. Most people have forgotten my accomplishments. However, now I have a proverbial pot and not the kind you smoke.

I have something only a small percentage of the people of the world have, a college education. I received it by inheriting something even more peculiar than addiction. I am a member of the Church of Jesus Christ of Latter-day Saints.

My Grandma Lilly converted to the Gospel of Jesus Christ and gave me the tools I needed to accomplish everything I ever dreamed of. I admire her inexpressible courage. I am so very grateful for her faith in me.

She left me no money when she died. That kind of thing feels like gambling as if the deceased is placing their last bet. Since I don't gamble, I'm not holding my breath.

No one ever bet on me, not like that anyway. I think those who truly love me are the people in my life who spent their days and nights praying for me, sacrificing for me, and encouraging me. They are the ones I have to thank. Their good gifts are worth passing on.

Of all the things God can do, I'm convinced that discovering wealth is the easiest. He knows where everything is. Wisdom is probably the next easiest because he knows everything and how it will end. All we have to do is listen.

Money and smarts don't do much for you without faith, hope, and charity. Faith is believing in something true and then keeping the corresponding commandment. Hope is only found in Jesus Christ. So, I cling to the good things I've been taught and am grateful for the gifts I've been given.

The pure love of Christ is the definition of charity. Mysterious as it may be, such love is also in my DNA. It duels with addiction for possession of my soul. So far, love wins.

Love triumphs when I mention my husband. It took forever to find him. Though I may lose him sooner than I should, he will never truly be lost because we chose eternity.

Married in the Holy Temple for time and all eternity, we brought five children into this beautiful and terrible world. Each one is a joy. Each one is our treasure. If nothing else rises with us when we die, except them, then that will be enough. My family is enough, but I want all of them, all of us.

The human family is wrapped in DNA and tied to time like a train on tracks. We move ahead. I, however, want no one obliterated by the train's passing.

So, I choose differently. When the tests of life offer A, B, or C, I choose none of the above. Instead, I rise above.

I'm not lazy. I'm not content. I want "all my Father hath." I'm willing to put forth every effort I possibly can to obtain those blessings for me and my children.

Yet, I understand it isn't enough. I, without the Lord, am nothing. I can do nothing alone. Or in other words, everything I do dies, never to rise again.

Everything I've ever accomplished has only to be forgotten for it to cease to exist. Forget me and I'm gone. Those who remember me already dwindle in number. Someday there will be none. My only hope is in Christ's mercy and grace.

Jesus Christ is powerful to save and can redeem me. He has redeemed me already. Wash as I may the mud in my DNA cannot become clean without Him.

So, I remember Him and keep His commandments that I may have his Spirit to be with me. The Spirit of God purifies. And as He raises me from the gutter of my genetic inheritance, I am made whole, receiving every blessing as if I had been born into them. I become a child of God.

I decided long ago whom I would serve and that made all the difference. How likely now am I to throw it away? After such a great price has been paid and so many miracles have been witnessed, what could cause me to roll back into the mud? One drink. One smoke. One pill. One unkind thought. One choice?

Sometimes that's all it takes. Sometimes we were born out of luck, and all we have is the determination of our soul on our side. Sometimes we must fight to have a choice at all. That's okay. Fight! With God all things are possible.

Dazzled

Sunshine on water dazzles my eyes more fully than gold and diamonds.

The cold and the lifeless are poor substitutes for a babbling brook.

Standing beneath the wind-rustled cottonwood leaves,

On a sunny, mountain slope at 45 degrees,

A brilliant world falls at my feet.

Origin of Inspiration

When you live in the desert of Southern, Utah, finding lush green vegetation and running water feeds your thirsty soul. As a child of the sun and a lover of water, I should have been thrilled when my parents informed me that we were taking a long hike into a box canyon. However, I was less than happy and could not imagine anything could make the early rise or long car ride worthwhile.

The dusty campground where we parked our green Dodge Dart was bleak. Pitching our tent was hot work. Why had we come all this way?

"There's a waterfall. So, wear your swimsuits under your T-shirt and shorts." Mom always had good advice for my little brother and me, though I was already too old to admit that.

I'm pretty sure I tried to wear flip-flops, but Dad shot them down.

"It's a long hike. You need good shoes." He was tall and dark-haired, not at all like my redheaded mother and me.

The only shoes I remember from childhood were a pair of blue and orange kangaroo shoes with a zipper pouch on the side. But that's a story for another day. I put on some tennis shoes and carried my kindergarten graduation gift, a round canteen.

We started our hike at ten in the morning. Despite my hat, the sun was already searing my fair skin like a steak. I had beef on the brain because Dad had told us the box Canyon was used historically to corral cattle. I found that profoundly prosaic.

We hiked along the left-hand wall of the canyon on a barren sandy trail. Red sandstone towered above us. Dad pointed out rock features and points of interest. It piqued my interest.

As we hiked further into the canyon, the vegetation sprang up beside a meandering, often branching, stream in the middle. Green grasses and small saplings added relief to the landscape and soothed my sun-dazzled eyes. Dad explained there weren't any big trees because the canyon flooded often and washed them away. Imagining that added a thrill of danger to the expedition for me.

The vegetation thickened. Birds and butterflies caught my attention with their blue or yellow animation. I wanted to go exploring, but even in the 1980s, we weren't permitted off the sparsely populated trail.

"There it is." Mom pointed ahead of us.

Being shorter than her, I couldn't see until we hiked closer. I heard it first, an ever-intensifying roar. My skin gave me the biggest clue when it beaded with perspiration, a rare occurrence in the arid climate. I marveled at the moisture glistening on my arm because I had never encountered much humidity during my ten years.

Unprepared for the grandeur of the falls, the power and magnitude swept over me. The rush of sound and the cascade of water through a waterworn edge at the head of the canyon blasted mist for a great distance. Invigorated, I raced ahead of my family.

The vision I encountered next, inspired me to write the novel *Woman of the Stone*. The crystal-clear pool at the waterfall's base captivated me completely. Wet with overspray, I stared as inspiration illuminated my imagination.

My blond, little brother sped ahead. He shucked his shoes, socks, and shirt on the smooth sand beach to venture a toe into the water. He wasn't a confident swimmer like me.

"We'll take a swim and then have lunch." Dad had carried a backpack with our picnic inside.

We swam. We ate. We hiked back to the campground and slept, but I was never the same.

Stay

Black consonants and vowels,
Separated on the rectangular box of a page,
Change translucent,
After a romp through crimson leaves.
They pale completely,
When children's laughter calls attention to a life best lived
now.
Yet, unless captured,
Those moments fade from memory and the heart.
Once poignant experiences,
Cease to have the savor of a crisp autumn day at play.
So, write, record, capture away,
Because the things we love don't stay.

Universe Created

One lazy, summer afternoon when I was a teenager, my family went fishing. We each chose a spot along the bank of Cedar Creek, not far from our Missouri home. I climbed on an overhanging tree and cast my line in the current.

My bobber drifted downstream to rest in the placid water along the shoreline. No fish bit. So, I relaxed.

I pulled a sleeve of crackers from my backpack. Casting again, I munched until my mouth became dry. With my cheeks packed, I let the crumbs fall on the still water.

I thought to attract fish. Instead, I witnessed something remarkable. The crumbs expanded in a circular pattern of swirling systems that imitated the universe.

I marveled at the tiny solar systems rotating in their orbits. The crumbs fell due to gravity and dispersed along the water's surface because of surface tension to cause the phenomenon. Pondering the significance, I abandoned my fishing pole and leaned against the tree to gaze at the sky.

It was a spiritual experience, as simple as Newton's apple. The breath of God created the universe. God obeys natural laws, all of which were spiritual first.

One day, scientists will explain the formation of the universe in such easy-to-understand terms that we will be forced to say to ourselves, "Why didn't I think of that?"

Colors

I've always admired the French and their rose-colored glasses. It's wild to see the world as you wish it, regardless of reality. I guess it means that in France, pink is the only color.

The Spanish speakers of the world have it great, too. There are so many vibrant hues that roll off the tongue. Azul. Amarillo. It's a thrill just to meet them, shake their hands and rub shoulders.

I hail from the home of the brave and bleed red, white, and blue. I've always lived free. So, why then am I stuck in this bleak color scheme?

Staring out the window at the gray on a rainy afternoon, I breathe in the stale air. I detect a hint of cardboard, nothing new. In the distance, a rumble rolls through the house boding excitement.

Just a tremor, nothing more. It's been years since I've seen real action. Broken, I've been stuffed away to live out the rest of my usefulness without purpose. I have friends in the same boat. All of us sailing nowhere.

True colors in a black and white world are one thing, but when everything has gone gray, where does that leave me? I imagine myself a pert sort of green, vibrant like grass. My hand twitches as if I can feel freshly mowed lawn at a picnic under the blazing, yellow sun. A tree. A bird in the sky. I've seen it all. It's not the same when viewed through a window.

The rumbling shakes the foundations of the house. I guess that's what it takes to hear a voice say the words I long to hear.

"Why don't you color?"

The lid rips off my box. Wild swirls and strokes. Sideways rubs. A masterpiece.

The Forest

Touch the trees when your heart is listening.
Watch the leaves when the light is glistening.
Hear the wind when the branches are whistling.
That is the feeling, sight, and sound of the forest.

Aspen Leaves

Gravel roads paved in gold,
play peekaboo with mountains.
Aspen leaves shimmer,
like sequins on Mother Nature's gown.
The rustling of leaves in a breeze
enchants like the tinkling of crystal.
Forests give glory to God,
more profoundly than cathedrals.
Nature's leaves tell stories across time.
I desire to read.

Holidays

The heater finally warmed the inside of the car. With one frozen hand I stripped off my stocking cap, ran my fingers through my hair, and grabbed the wheel again. Snow slapped against the windshield, and the car slid in the slush.

"Who drives in weather like this," I said.

I tightened my grip on the wheel. Focusing my attention on the bumper in front of me, I hoped the car directly behind me wouldn't lose control. On the radio, the commercial break finally ended and of all things, a Christmas carol played.

"Oh, brother! Everyone's a comedian."

I glared at the radio for a bit and then stared at the road. Before I knew it, I had a headache. I'd forgotten to stop glaring, and now because of my throbbing temples, I couldn't stop.

As the third Christmas song played, I shut off the radio. Commercialism destroyed other holidays. My disgust with greed lulled as silence filled my car. The rush of warm air from the heater eased my headache, and I relaxed against the seat.

"Over the river and through the woods to—" To my astonishment, I laughed at the childhood memories my song brought to mind.

Apple pie and turkey filled my happy thoughts. The snow quit falling, and the road thinned of cars. I smiled, pulled off the main road, and parked the car in front of my parents' house.

With a contented sigh, I braced myself to open the door and face the cold. Hopping out into the snow, I hurried across the white yard to the door. Before I reached it, I smelled dinner.

It brought me up short. "That smells so good."

I took a deep breath and smiled big. As I breathed the cold air, I realized how amazing fresh snow smells. I memorized the moment, mixing my awe with a wave of warm emotion as my eyes filled with beauty and my heart swelled with gratitude.

"Thank you," I whispered to the sky.

It felt good to be grateful. Stomping my feet, I took the last few steps onto the porch and opened the screen. Just then the door flew wide.

"Happy Thanksgiving!" My beaming brother filled the doorway partially blocking the view of the festive holiday scene in our parents' home. "Nice hair."

Powder Play

Snow is softly falling gently through the trees.
Powder's dry and light midway to your knees.
See the breath of morning floating on the breeze?
I am in the dawning of the day, pleased.

Mist on the Lake

Hugging the curves of the scenic route through King Jack Park in my red Chrysler car, I hurried to convey my two girls to elementary school. They needed to be on time. I needed to see the lake.

Late Autumn gray cloaked the overcast landscape in early morning precipitation. Through the trees, the Praying Hands Memorial came into view. The lake beside it peeked between the trees and I stopped the car.

Mist on the lake. What shall I bake? A smile curved my lips to see the wisps of moisture sweep the limestone cliffs to cross the flat gray surface of the water. Blueberry muffins.

I put the car in gear and drove the girls to school.

The afternoon held the delights of baking. I inhaled with satisfaction the aroma of muffins fresh from the oven. I normally wasn't the kind of mom to do such things. However, the cozy feelings invoked by the morning drive had me inspired.

Picking the girls up from school through the hustle and hubbub of Webb City traffic at that particular hour of the day wasn't something I looked forward to. Stressed to the max by the drivers on cellphones, I avoided mayhem with my mad driving skills. With both girls buckled in the back, we were off to the park.

At least the sun was shining.

Zoom, zoom, whoosh! I cut the engine and tossed muffins into the back seat. Silence...mostly.

In my spot by the lake, I drank in the depths of nature's draught. Aquamarine waters winked at me in the sunshine, waving with the breeze. The tall trunks of trees held firm as their branches creaked with each gust. Their last leaves glided to the surface of my joy.

How could I comprehend then that anyone could take away a lake? Who would want it anyway? It wasn't even a lake really. It was an enormous mineshaft or strip pit, and less than worthless to anyone but those who clung to it for renewal.

At first, there were rumors. The EPA. The EPA. Town meeting today. City Council. What will they say? They're cleaning up the chat. Hooray!

Who cares?

The winter farmers market on a fine Saturday morning in the park held many wonders. Music. Friends. Giant checkers.

"Girls sit on Santa's lap. I need a picture." Click! Click! "Thank you, Mrs. Claus. I love your hugs."

"Have you heard?" she asked.

I shook my head as I tracked my children. They sat at a picnic table to glue Styrofoam ornaments together. Active kids. Crafty.

"The EPA plans to fill the lake with chat." Mrs. Claus said.

Leveled, I turned to her agape. Mind stalled, it seemed like time stood still. And then a gear in my brain caught and my teeth ground.

"They want us all to drink that stuff?" I asked.

Mrs. Claus's cherubic face scrunched in confusion. "What do you mean?"

I pointed through the plastic windows of the vinyl pavilion covers. "The water tower is only a couple hundred yards from the lake. Half the city's runoff collects here, there's no outlet, yet the lake stays fresh year-round."

She still looked at me in question.

"It feeds the aquifer," I said. "Thousands of people drink it. Where did you think the water went?"

Mrs. Claus, the picture of alarm. "Oh! That won't do. I'll tell my sister."

"We'd better tell everyone." I shook my head, hoping someone else had thought of this.

The edge of fear tainted my every drive through the park.

Around the area, enormous equipment loaded chat onto railway cars. Whew! Vast swaths of barren piles were cleared by black smoke bellowing beasts. It began to look like earth again.

And then it happened.

Load by load, the lake dried up. Tree by tree, the bulldozers had their day. Until the lake had gone away.

Now. My girls are in high school. We've moved from there. A bit of heaven on this green planet is where we stay. Trees and grass. A pond.

It's not the same. It's better. But on farmer's market day, we go to town.

Beside the Praying Hands is a wide field. There are no footprints in the sparse grass. A suspicious dip in the marshy middle is the only clue to those who don't know that something isn't right.

The EPA had their day. No people have two heads. Hooray!

But I pity the man who mows it. I hope they give him hazard pay. Though, perhaps that would give away the thing I've failed to mention.

Because at least one of us hopes the field will wash away. The chat will flush! And from the sinkhole will form a lake with trees growing up to conceal from the world nature's gift to those who care.

American Color Wheel

I find it wrong when gangs lay claim to colors, causing people to fear wearing anything but black and white. I grew tall in Sacramento, California. In the 1980s we wore neon colors and acid wash jeans with jelly bracelets. But gangs abounded, and the colors red and blue were shunned by everyday people.

The diversity of our skin's tones had been blotted out or painted over with the ink of tattoos, the crude offerings of man's hand.

Now even the color black is taken by a flag. Terrorism is its message; written in white letters we cannot read. Yet, the meaning is death.

So, I push back. No one owns the rainbow. Your symbols were my colorful world first. Back off! Let me see, free.

Sailor's End

Bloody ribbons of valor,
The siren sea's uniform.
Draped and on display,
A floating gallery of gore.

Resolution

I see life in metaphors, always working a puzzle in my head. I gravitate toward those people who never solve theirs. My Uncle Chuck is one such man, a military veteran with issues, but this is not his story.

Recently, I met Veteran Ronald C. Mosbaugh who served as a corpsman (medic) on a thirteen-month tour in Vietnam. He has written numerous stories about his time in the service that have moved me.

The accounts were written as therapy for his PTSD (post-traumatic stress disorder). They are a means of achieving some degree of PTG (post-traumatic growth). The accounts astounded me, but one account stood out in its detail and its haunting effect on the man who wrote it. More emotion came through because he still doesn't understand it, and that speaks to me.

Ron wrote about his memory of two "buddies" assigned to his platoon. One of them was shot, and the other led an enraged charge on a small village. Every living thing was killed.

"What does it take to kill an old man?" was spoken by the grief-stricken buddy who had killed an older Vietnamese man in a gruesome manner.

The words echo into the present. I've read about veterans committing suicide in large numbers. I've lost several classmates who served in the military.

So, I too pose the question, "What does it take to kill a man?"

I think it is his younger self leveling his weapon on his older self and pulling the trigger. The expectation that age and wisdom should be able to solve the problems of the past dog the older man. He dodges the figurative bullet for as long as he can until something more concrete ends his fight or flight panic mode. Sometimes it's suicide.

There is no escaping from one's self, but a form of resolution is possible. I posit this thought. The "buddy" killed in action, the enraged friend leading the charge, the followers who also committed the act of vengeance, and the old man who took three hits to kill and died without a word spoken are all the same man who dies today of his psychological wounds.

I think that's why the details of the atrocity stood out in Corpsman Mosbaugh's mind and remain unresolved today. He needs to survive the mental bullet that his mind fired years ago. Contrary to human instinct, this kind of mental bullet cannot be survived by dodging it.

No one can run forever. One must stand like a man at a mark and be prepared to take the hit. The impact of facing it is to heal, not to maim. Though, one cannot fully realize that until one accepts it.

Corpsman Mosbaugh seems to feel responsible for everything that happened around him in Vietnam, but the burden is not his alone. He had little if any control over the actions of others. He can hand it to the Lord.

We have the opportunity to kneel before our Father in Heaven. We can be washed clean by the blood of Christ. If blood requires blood, then let it be the blood of our Savior and Redeemer, Jesus Christ our Lord. The price has already been paid.

Shades of Blue

Every shade and hue of blue reminds me of a rendezvous.
Cast aside the red rock climbing, a hidden park is oh so charming.
A writer in a writing mood, I met my hero here today.
Pen in hand, I had a plan, but heroes lead where no one can.
We fought the dragon, sailed the sea, and then we...
Looked beyond the blue.
My soul bespoke a sonnet true.
Of love. Of life. Of me and you.
Darkness falls upon the land.
My picnic lays upon the sand.
Uneaten sandwich. Unopened soda.
Unplanned, yet oh so grand.
Still, I dream beside a stream,
My stories gleam bright as the stars.
My hope one day is to see Mars.
Or visit a green, inviting gable.
The lands of books past, present, and future,
Live inside a well-shelved soul.
Treasures of a lifetime reading,
Are gifts to me without repeating.

Virgin River

On a warm summer's day, my mother, her friend Jan, Jan's two-year-old daughter Kristin, my little brother Heath, and I headed out for a swim. The river flowed deceptively calm. We exited the car and descended the bank near a fifteen-foot waterfall in the southwestern corner of Utah.

The muddy water flowed over a dam to create the waterfall. We swam in the large pool above the dam. It was a popular place, but today we were the only ones there. If we were careful, then we'd be just fine, Mom said.

I was an adventurous soul, and my brother always tagged along. We were a team, but I was the fearless leader. I had learned to swim when I was two years old. That made me a five-year veteran of the water. My little brother was afraid and still hadn't learned to swim.

We splashed and played for a while. I guess a lot of time passed because just having fun and being curious wasn't enough for me anymore. I needed some danger.

While exploring the muddy water with my feet, I found a peculiar drop-off. It was near the waterfall, but not close enough that I couldn't easily swim against the current. I guarded the secret cautiously. I had a feeling I could use it to create some mischief.

In the shallows, my brother chased tadpoles and minnows. He would never be able to catch any. I could show off by catching a few, but I had something better in mind. With a casual look over at Mom to assure me that she hadn't detected my intentions, I inconspicuously walked through the waist-high water over to my brother.

"Heath, come and look at what I found!" I made my voice sound excited.

The bait was cast. He bit without hesitation. Unsuspecting, he followed me through the water to the trap I had set.

"Hurry up," I spoke in my normal condescending and impatient tone.

I let him pass me just in time for him to go over the underwater drop-off. He plunged into the depths. I had slyly stopped short of doing the same, but I didn't even have time to laugh at my fine joke before I realized something had gone wrong.

He didn't come up as fast as I thought he would. The Virgin River's current, which had seemed so gentle earlier, now pulled at me with great strength. When he did surface, he was a lot further away from me and closer to the dam than I'd imagined possible. Terrified, he gasped for air and would have gone under again except that I had already leaped into action.

I dove after him and before he went under the second time, I was behind him and had my arm over his left shoulder and under his right arm. I kicked my legs with all my strength. We were still moving toward the waterfall. It seemed an eternity that I remained undecided as to which action I ought to take to save our lives.

The bank stretched ten feet away. The dam was an ever-shrinking distance of about twenty-five feet from us. A gracious willow drooped peacefully over the surface of the river on our side of the falls.

None of this information offered me an escape. The willow's branches were not, and I calculated would never be, within reach. I doubted that they would support us even if we could have grabbed them.

We continued drifting backward toward a fifteen-foot drop onto jagged rocks. There was no way out. Mom was going to find out what I had done.

I called for help. My voice sounded calm, demanding, and reasonable. I don't know how I remained so cool and collected.

Mom answered by looking downstream in our direction. She responded with immediate and dazzling speed. Running through the shallow water, she dove directly for us.

She swam the thirty feet, slid behind us, placed her hands on our backs, and launched us with great force toward the river bank. Her long legs had pushed off from a log that stuck up from the bottom. The momentum of that push took us to safety.

We huddled together on the river's slippery edge until Mom joined us. She gathered us in her arms and hugged us both. She told me that I had saved my brother's life.

She actually thought I was a heroine. I never told her it was my fault in the first place. I was too ashamed to admit it.

Bits of Nothing

I write upon the dead trunks of trees, paper dry and ink wet.

Wannabe.

Press me softly lest I fail to tell the tale of a rising sea and a windy gale.

Trite.

Preferring failure, I digress, becoming loathe to put forth a single word.

Quitter.

I am surrounded by leaves, the litter of trees, my words reduced to shreds.

Waste.

I write nothingness, hiding in the branches of my mind.

Coward.

My will is not still. My hope flickers in the breeze.

Obsessed.

Forcefully tattooing my grief and love on nature's page, I mar myself.

Fool.

Forests hewn and ground to bits, I consume them by my hand.

Drain.

Undisciplined.

The volumes of my mind's fruit are consumed, leaving nothing.

Stretch Limousine

At the age of seventeen, I graduated early from El Dorado Springs R-II High School in rural Missouri. Immediately recruited by the DeVry Institute of Technology, I moved to Kansas City. I sought my fortune as an engineering major at the state-of-the-art school. Poverty, at least after college, was no longer in my plans.

Spring of 1993, my parents drove me to Kansas City. I enrolled and moved into student housing at a nearby apartment complex. My dad used the phonebook to find the local chapel. Since it was Wednesday night, the bishop was available to meet us there.

The drive was an easy distance. However, I wouldn't have a car. My parents worried because it was too far to walk to the church building.

The bishop said, "I'll arrange for Brother Moore to pick you up. Roger and his family are good people, and their daughter is just a little older than you."

We thanked the bishop and left his office.

My dad said, "Roger Moore is the name of an actor who played James Bond."

Mom and Dad departed for home, leaving me on my own for the first time in my life. When Sunday rolled around, I showered and put on a dress. Then, I waited right by the door for my ride.

My three new roommates lounged around the living room in their pajamas, bonding over reruns on television. A single, crisp, ring of the bell came at last. I answered the door.

"Your car has arrived," said a tall chauffeur in full dress uniform, including the shiny black shoes and gray hat.

This attracted my roommates' attention. They hopped up and raced behind me down the hallway to look out the window. The man descended the three flights of stairs as I followed him in wide-eyed silence.

When we rounded the corner, my jaw dropped. There, shining in the sun, was a stretch limousine. It was flawless and glossy black.

The distinguished-looking driver in his gray suit opened the door without a word. Astonished, I sat in the vast, empty backseat. He closed the door and drove us to the chapel.

That was Brother Moore. He was on call, hence his being dressed for the job and having the car. Each week repeated the same way, though the limousines often changed colors. Sometimes they were new and sometimes they were old, but they were always shiny on the outside even if the upholstery occasionally sagged or had cigarette burns and frequently smelled of smoke.

I remember riding past the Piggly Wiggly. Without fail, more than one person stopped to stare with their grocery bag suspended in midair as they loaded their items into their car. People watched me go by like I was Madonna. I watched them with equal wonderment, thinking, *I'm still just me*.

I had been excited about earning an engineering degree because I would make a good living. I loved science, but I needed to be rich. Somehow, those Sunday drives changed my mind.

I quit caring about making lots of money. I figured I'd rather earn respect than buy it. I'd rather be as clean on the inside as I was on the outside. I'd rather have God love me than the people of the world admire me. So, thank you, Bishop and Brother Moore. You changed my life.

Crocodile Style

I loved climbing rocks as a kid, and rappelling always appealed to me. My first opportunity to try it arose in 1994 at Missouri Southern State College in Joplin, Missouri. Walking to the dorms after the last day of class in May on a sunny afternoon, I noticed students streaming across the grass to the police academy tower and followed after them.

Most people stood around watching a couple of others learn to rappel. However, I tossed my backpack in the dust at the bottom and hiked the one-sided tower's open, wooden staircase. The activity was free as part of a campus-wide summer break and commencement celebration. It was a perfect way for me to unwind after a stressful year.

At the top of the tower, the instructor helped me into the climbing harness. He clipped me to the line with a locking carabiner. Then, he backed me to the edge of the platform.

"Hold the rope here and here." He showed me where, then yelled to the man holding my rope at the bottom, "On belay!"

As I looked down, the four-story tower seemed to grow tenfold taller.

"On rappel!" The tiny man at the bottom cupped his hands around his mouth like a megaphone.

"Now ease backward until you're perpendicular to the planks on the wall." The instructor caught my eye and held my attention. "Lean back, a little more, good, now let some rope go, good. Just sit down, more, a bit more. See! Now you're going to jump as you loosen your grip on the rope and hop to the bottom."

My knees trembled, but his gaze remained steady. Because of his easy smile, I jumped. It was an absolute thrill to conquer my newly formed adult inhibitions. I felt as free as a kid again and landed on my feet in the dirt without a splinter or a scrape.

"Good job, kid. Just like a pro," said the man on belay. He clapped me on the shoulder and then helped me out of the harness. "You going again?"

"Yes, sir!" I hiked the tower and rappelled twice more without a second thought.

On my fourth time at the top, the instructor asked me, "Want to go Aussie style?"

"What's that?"

"Australian rappel is when you go down the wall facing forward."

My eyebrows shot upward as my smile brightened, "Absolutely!"

The world stretched before me toward the lush, green horizon. I held the rope at my hip and leaned over the tower platform. Adjusting my footing until the soles of my sneakers rested on the top plank of the police tower, I enjoyed the anticipation.

Releasing some rope, I jumped until I landed squarely with both feet on the ground. The man on belay's grin couldn't have been bigger. He helped me unhook, and I hiked the zig-zag stairwell again.

The instructor flashed me a toothy expression of approval. "All right, now that you've gone down the wall a few times, are you ready to go off an open side? Aussie style?"

I laughed as I leaned over to look off one of the three sides without any wooden planks forming a wall. "You bet!"

"You do this, and I'm going to have to call you Crocodile."

I beamed with enthusiasm at the reference to the fearless, Australian hero in a popular movie called Crocodile Dundee. So, I belted the harness on over my hip-hugging Levis, clipped on the line, yelled "On belay!", leaned out, and leaped into the air.

Butterflies Bite

Social butterflies are society's sharks.
Move.
Circle.
Bite.
Just a tip from one butterfly to another.

Comedic Profile

I have been profiled by the police on a few occasions. I've lived in Sacramento, Kansas City, Seoul, outside of Joplin, just to name a few places. I've never been robbed.

Poor translates.

Admittedly, there's not a lot of robbing going on in Seoul, South Korea. However, a chubby, golden-headed gal with incredible noonsups (that's the little crease in your eyelids) garners a lot of attention. Not all of it is ideal.

Years ago, I was in South Korea for eighteen months serving a mission for the Church of Jesus Christ of Latter-day Saints. I had a Book of Mormon in my hand and a Korean companion at my side. We were walking back to the apartment one evening when a little old man grabbed ahold of my arm.

"I'm taking you home with me," he said in Korean as he tried to compel me down the street.

Now, he was drunk, and I was more than a foot taller than him. I weighed a bit more than him. We'll say five pounds more than him. Okay, maybe it was five kilos more. All right, I weighed an entire sack of rice more than him. Most Koreans can't lift one, with the possible exception of stewardesses for Asiana Air.

So, I wasn't worried.

I politely declined his offer and gently removed his hand. I felt like apologizing because he seemed so devastated. As we walked to our apartment, my companion explained the situation a little better for me. The man wanted to bring an American into his home to save face with his wife so she wouldn't yell at him for being drunk.

Trust me, that kind of admiration is not the kind of attention I have received from the American Police when I drive any car I've ever owned. I've been profiled my whole life, but when they pull me over and find me sitting in the driver's seat, they're not thinking, "I wonder what she's been up to," they're thinking, "I hope she doesn't ask for my number."

My thoughts are often, "But Officer, I have amazing noonsups!"

My Day in Potter's Clay

I mold my day like potter's clay.
Tight at the base,
stretching to take in the light,
striving hard to make it stay,
yet as it fades,
I draw inward,
arms folded,
heart turned upward,
open to the sky.

Bittersweet

I approached him on the train station platform in South Korea. He stood in a space cushion an amazing three meters in diameter. In December's harsh clarity, he held his hands inside the pockets of his black overcoat. He looked tired, more than he had three months ago.

Events had come together in such a way as to give us a few moments to talk before our trains arrived. This kind of chance rarely occurred and felt like an opportunity. Despite this, I hesitated to go to him until my overwhelming need for encouragement won out. There was no other American available to talk to.

"How are things in Incheon?" I asked because making small talk about a missionary-safe topic seemed like the right way to start.

"Good," he said. "You served in Incheon about a year ago, didn't you?"

Flattered that he remembered such a small detail about me, I answered, "Yes, but not in the same Ward as you. Are you transferring today?"

It didn't matter a whole lot, but I was curious. I would remain in my area with a new companion for one month. Then I'd return home to a small town in Missouri.

"No," he said. "How about you?"

"No. Sister Reckling transferred. I'll be serving with Sister Ye Eun Jeong. The house will be all Korean for Christmas, except for me."

He didn't respond but seemed to understand.

"It's going to be tough." I wanted to be sure he had indeed understood the ramifications of my spending another holiday here.

He knew as well as I did that they did things differently in Korea than in the United States. Why didn't he say something funny or helpful? Crazy as it seemed, I was struggling.

"Your mission has been tough from the beginning." The icy wind made him squint his blue eyes as he stared along the tracks.

"Yes." It was true.

I tucked away my disappointment at his unsympathetic response. We stood in silence for a few moments. Then, my train approached the platform.

"I have to go," I said.

"Sugohaseyo." He made eye contact and bowed slightly, telling me to work hard.

"Sugohaseyo." I glanced at him and bowed as well, but I needed to hurry.

More than that, I was angry with him for always keeping the rules so strictly. I needed help, and he had refused to be helpful. I couldn't fault him, it was how things had to be, but for once it really bothered me. For pity's sake if nothing else, he could have been more sympathetic.

I took the three strides to the other Sister Missionaries. My new companion and I gathered her luggage and boarded the train. Setting the bags inside the train car, sudden movement caused me to grab a strap and hold on. I glanced out the windows. He was looking at me.

When Sister Ye and I arrived at our apartment, I told her I needed a nap. Folding out my "yo" on the floor, I wrapped in my quilt and covered my face. I didn't sleep but cried quietly. My companion provided the only privacy available in the room by studying at her desk while she pretended not to notice that anything was amiss with me.

Patience is the Creator's Wisdom

Good people come and hear,
The story of a girl from near
That traveled far to find a man.
Looking, looking for to find
A man to marry who is refined.
She found a tall and handsome man.
Are you the man I've come to find?
Not I, he said, you are too plain.
Listening, listening for to hear
A man to marry who sings clear.
She found a man who sings at weddings.
Are you the man I've come to find?
Not I, he said, you make me cry.
Feeling, feeling for to find
A man to marry who is kind.
She found a tender gentleman.
Are you the man I've come to find?
Not I, he said, you shun your kind.
Weeping, weeping far and wide
A man to marry, she could not find.
In the quiet of the morning,
She found a sunrise orange and bright.
Within her heart, she saw the light.

Smiling, smiling far and wide
She saw the wonders of the Earth.
In an orchard filled with birds,
She heard a melody from above,
And her breast filled with the song.
Singing, singing far and wide,
She praised the maker all the time.
In a town quite full of men,
She saw him laboring with his might.
When he stumbled, she took his hand.
Helping, helping this one man,
She felt the love she'd come to find.

She Cries

On the first night home with our daughter, she cries her newborn cry. We smile and smother her with attention. She dozes off at the breast. Daddy goes to bed.

I rock her, looking at her milk-white features and her thick dark hair. She's beautiful. Rocking up out of the chair, I take her to her crib.

With one soft kiss on her forehead, I lay her down. She cries. I return with her to the rocking chair.

She spits up on both of us. It seems like a lot of milk. We're soaked.

At the changing table in her room, I ever so carefully strip her to the skin. I wash her, dress her, and wrap her in a new receiving blanket. She screams through it all.

I lay her in the crib, run to put the laundry in the washer, strip my pajamas off and toss them in too. Then I race to my room for new PJs and return to pick her up. My husband's still asleep.

In my arms, she's still crying. Soothing tones. Bouncy walk. She calms and is just fussy now.

Rocking chair gliding along, elbows falling asleep, nipples getting sore, third pair of pajamas tonight, I notice that the sun is rising. The shower comes on. The baby is dozing at my breast.

My husband kisses me on the cheek. "I'll see you tonight."

Our baby cries, but daddy has to go to work. She cries until she's sick. We're soaked again. Good thing thirty people came to the baby shower.

New PJs for baby, a T-shirt for me, and the laundry is going again. I close the blinds. T-shirts need trap doors. I toss it off and rock the baby. She cries in her sleep with her lip trembling, melting me.

The doctor says, "She looks healthy."

Baby smiles at him.

"She cries a lot," I say.

"Babies cry." The doctor makes a note. "I want to see her again in two weeks."

The sand-colored carpet in the living room is turning dark in splotches. I'm too tired to care. Dinner is on the table. The baby fell asleep thirty minutes ago, for the first time today.

Daddy comes in the door. Kisses. Dinner. Sex. Bed.

Baby cries. Daddy gets her. They play. She coos.

Projectile vomit and a screaming baby. Showering daddy. I take the baby and do it all again.

I'm in the rocking chair, boobs bared, baby nursing the air as she lays in my lap. Daddy chuckles softly. Kisses my forehead startling me awake. Baby cries.

"Have a good day, Honey," my husband says.

He opens the front door and walks to the company van. The door swings shut. I reach over and lock it.

Dawn on the horizon is the first sunlight I've seen in days. I nurse the baby and lie her down. Miracle!

I start the clothes drier, eat, and down a glass of water. My head hits the pillow, and I fall into blissful oblivion. Baby cries. It's been twenty-seven minutes.

Refinement

Refinement isn't a word used very often anymore. If you are picturing an oil refinery, then my point is made. What does it matter how refined or genteel I or anyone is these days?

The era where it mattered is gone, right? Intellect has been replaced by intelligence on paper. Gentility has been supplanted by dollars in the bank. Sensibility has been thrown out for practicality.

This brings us to a chaotic state of idleness interspersed with activity, where everything is in vain. Do I receive brownie points in life when I read Shakespeare? Perhaps I'm given a sideways glance, but not credit for improving my mind or appreciating a genius of human understanding on a deeper level.

In fact, if I use my judgment in any form, I'm frowned upon because these days hedonism abounds. Striving to improve one's life is secretly thought to be pointless. Behind the laughter of the populace exists a fear of not having a dependable future. That fear forces manic laughter from hopeless youth and adults alike.

Save money? Why? Every day our currency loses value.

Attend college? Why? Every day the price goes up.

The temptations of today erode the staying power of students even as the job market shrinks and the prospects of fortune fade. Remain a child as long as the pity of society permits it because life will collide with the lifestyle all too soon and the lies believed will be dispelled before long. So, "eat drink and be merry for tomorrow we die and all shall be well".

What other choice do I have? Nothing is easier than giving up. However, one option exists that is far more rewarding on a personal level, refinement. Investing in myself doesn't take money, or at least very little in today's world.

So much of what I need to know to improve myself is available via the internet. Anyone can learn to sing, play the piano, speak another language, knit, sew, paint, write, take stunning photographs, manage finances, and even earn a living online. Nearly anything I can imagine learning is available for next to nothing.

What the world cannot teach me is a desire to become refined. My role models are lifted so far aloft that accomplishing similar feats feels impossible. Perhaps that kind of success is unattainable for the average person.

However, that kind of refinement isn't what I'm talking about. I'm referring to personal progress. Achievement leads to a sense of worth and confidence. Virtues can't be purchased. They're gifts from God.

God, you say? Yes, God. Without him in my life and society, I'm nothing. With him, I can do anything.

I'm his child, and I can be like him. If my mother were a doctor, then she would be pleased if I became a doctor. It would honor her that I followed in her footsteps, and I would be blessed forever that I had not chosen to play all day and work in the fast-food industry.

Would you like fries with that? No! No, I would not.

The fact that my mother stayed at home as much as possible and was always there for me growing up is no less admirable or worthy of my emulation. That's why I have followed her example. Homemaking is not the only thing I've done, but I've been here for my husband and children for many years now.

Being a stay-at-home mom isn't easy. As hard as it has been, however, there's no one else who could have done it as well as I have. I'm an indispensable part of my family.

I graduated from a university and speak four languages. I work a few evening hours a week, teaching English as a second language to adults at Crowder College. I've chosen to be a wife and mother, rather than to work more.

It will not always be so. One day my children will be grown. One day my husband may pass away. Then I will have time to do everything I wish.

What will I want more than anything in the world? I will want to be with my family forever. No other source promises this save God.

I value God above all else. He values me above his own life, above all suffering, above all sorrow, and beyond my current ability to comprehend. I trust him and in his love.

I believe him to be refined. Therefore, I refine myself to be like him out of admiration, respect, and love. The world is a better place because of refined individuals, families, and societies. Let's all be a part of that.

Retain Some Mystery

Cast not the windows of your soul too wide,
Lest the winds of this Earth steal the very heat from your
blood.
Retain some mystery,
For more renowned than Anonymous endures the Mona Lisa.

Don't miss out!

Visit the website below and you can sign up to receive emails whenever S.V. Farnsworth publishes a new book. There's no charge and no obligation.

https://books2read.com/r/B-A-LKBI-UBBWB

BOOKS 2 READ

Connecting independent readers to independent writers.

Did you love *Tucked Away in a Discolored Scrapbook: Creative Nonfiction with Poetry*? Then you should read *A Rare Connection: Inspirational Romantic Suspense*[1] by S.V. Farnsworth!

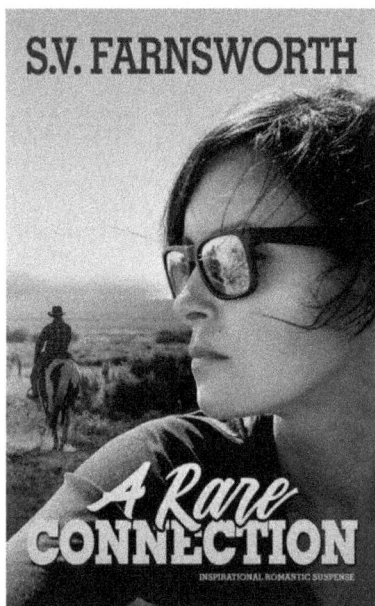

Read more at https://svfarnsworthauthor.com.

Also by S.V. Farnsworth

Fusion in a Fission World
Hard Start: Mars Intrigue
Tidal Pulse: Mars Revolution

Modutan Empire
Woman of the Stone
Monarch in the Flames

Standalone
A Rare Connection: Inspirational Romantic Suspense
Tucked Away in a Discolored Scrapbook: Creative Nonfiction
with Poetry

Watch for more at https://svfarnsworthauthor.com.

About the Author

Raised in a forest, S.V. Farnsworth thinks adventure is a cold steel knife in a leather sheath at her side. Nature rests her soul like nothing else. She often escapes across a meadow into the cover of the woods, finding comfort in sunlight filtered through a canopy of leaves. The closeness of trees speaks relief deeper than a cabin overlooking a hidden lake. If this is how you feel, then build your cabin across from hers and enjoy the world as friends.

S.V. Farnsworth writes immersive deep-shelf fiction with noble characters battling dark worlds. She enjoys resonant high fantasy, space opera, and romantic suspense novels. She teaches ESL for Crowder College in Neosho, Missouri.

Find her speaking at small gatherings and local book events. Discover exclusive short stories and updates for her novels at https://svfarnsworthauthor.com/newsletter if you see yourself in the rich language of her epic theme.

Read more at https://svfarnsworthauthor.com.

**Stone Wolfe
Press**

About the Publisher

Established in 2019, Stone Wolfe Press is an independent publisher that is pleased to have released both novels and nonfiction. Their published books include the following titles: *Woman of the Stone* (2019), *A Rare Connection: Inspirational Romantic Suspense* (2020), *Monarch in the Flames* (2020), *Hard Start: Mars Intrigue* (2021), and *Tucked Away in a Discolored Scrapbook: Creative Nonfiction with Poetry* (2022). The press strives to release two publications a year.

www.ingramcontent.com/pod-product-compliance
Lightning Source LLC
Chambersburg PA
CBHW051733040426
42447CB00008B/1107